T0009325

Who Is
Lionel Messi?

Who Is
Lionel Messi?

by James Buckley Jr.

illustrated by Manuel Gutierrez

Penguin Workshop

Por Los Renegados de Santa Bárbara—JB

A Lionel, a toda su familia, y a mi madre, Elsa,
que también amaba el fútbol—MG

PENGUIN WORKSHOP
An imprint of Penguin Random House LLC, New York

First published in the United States of America by Penguin Workshop,
an imprint of Penguin Random House LLC, New York, 2024

Visit us online at penguinrandomhouse.com.

Library of Congress Cataloging-in-Publication Data is available.

Printed in the United States of America

ISBN 9780593754825 (paperback)   10 9 8 7 6 5 4 3 2 1 CJKW
ISBN 9780593754832 (library binding)   10 9 8 7 6 5 4 3 2 1 CJKW

Contents

Who Is Lionel Messi? 1

From Argentina to Spain 6

Barcelona 16

Highs and Lows 27

Finally, a World Champion 34

Messi to Miami 42

Timelines 48

Bibliography 50

Who Is Lionel Messi?

All the fans in DRV PNK Stadium in Fort Lauderdale, Florida, were on their feet, cheering. Some had paid thousands of dollars for tickets to watch the last-place Inter Miami team play in the 2023 Major League Soccer (MLS) Leagues Cup. Most of those fans were cheering for the Miami team, which was tied 1–1 with Mexico's Cruz Azul. Miami needed a goal to avoid a penalty-kick shootout to advance in the tournament.

The man in the pink shirt with number ten on his back paid no attention to the fans. He was setting up to do something he did better than anyone else in soccer history. He stood a couple of yards behind the soccer ball. The eyes in his brown-bearded face stared at the goal, twenty-five yards away.

The referee blew his whistle. Lionel (say: LEE-oh-nell) Messi took a few steps toward the ball. His left leg whipped back, then forward. The ball zipped up and over a defensive wall of opponents and flew under the crossbar of

the goal. As it smacked into the back of the net, the Miami fans screamed for joy. Lionel Messi ran to hug his teammates. Then he went to the sidelines to embrace his three sons and his wife.

It was a shocking, amazing miracle shot. The game ended just seconds later; Inter Miami had beaten Cruz Azul 2–1.

Making magic on a soccer field was nothing new for Lionel Messi. When he arrived in June 2023 to play for Inter Miami, the team had won only five of its twenty-two games that year. Messi's first games with the team were in the Leagues Cup, a competition that didn't count toward the regular-season standings—so every team had a chance. But with Lionel, Inter Miami had more than just a chance. Already the winner of seven trophies as the world's best player, plus a 2022 World Cup trophy with Argentina, Lionel inspired his new team. Over the next month, he electrified world soccer. Stores ran out of replicas of his pink jersey as fans rushed to buy them. People packed stadiums to watch, millions tuned in on TV, celebrities arrived to see him play.

From almost the moment Lionel first touched a soccer ball as a boy, he had been thrilling everyone who watched. His skill and his hard work had taken him from his home in Argentina to success in Spain to the very top of the world of soccer. And then he went to the United States to create even more memories. Here's the story of how he did it.

CHAPTER 1
From Argentina to Spain

The world's greatest soccer player was born in a city that is obsessed with soccer. Lionel Andrés Messi was born on June 24, 1987, in Rosario, Argentina. Rosario is about 185 miles northwest of the capital, Buenos Aires. When Lionel was born, the city was home to about a dozen soccer clubs. One of the two biggest clubs was called Newell's Old Boys. Lionel's father, Jorge, had played for Newell's when he was younger. Lionel's oldest brother, Rodrigo, had also played there; his next older brother, Matías, played for a different club. When Lionel was three, he got his first soccer ball; it was red, one of Newell's team colors.

Using a nickname that some fans still use for

Lionel, Rodrigo later said, "Leo left the house with a ball, lived with the ball, and slept with the ball. He only wanted the ball."

By the time he was four, Lionel was dribbling that ball past his older brothers and most of the kids in the neighborhood. It didn't matter that he was very small for his age. He had what his father called "a gift" for playing soccer. Every Sunday, the Messi boys would gather at their grandmother Celia's house and play all afternoon before Celia made the family a big meal.

Jorge Messi worked for a steel company. Lionel's mother, who was also named Celia, was busy working, too. So it was his grandmother who first took Lionel to find a team when he was four years old. She walked with Lionel to Grandoli, a team that was practicing in their Las Heras neighborhood. The Grandoli coach thought that Lionel was too small, but Lionel's grandmother insisted. "Put him on, put him on," she said. From almost the first moment Lionel touched the ball on the small field, he was a star.

He dribbled past defenders, he made perfect passes, he scored goal after goal.

"She was my first fan at training, at the games. Her cries of encouragement were always with me," Lionel remembered about his grandmother.

While he played soccer for Grandoli, he did other things with his friends. They loved PlayStation video games and also played marbles on the sidewalks. One of his good friends was Antonela Roccuzzo, the cousin of his best friend. He made other friends among his Grandoli teammates.

On the soccer field, Lionel was the center of attention, but in school, he was very shy. In some classes, he asked friends to give answers rather than raise his own hand. In 1993, the Messi family welcomed a daughter, Maria Sol.

When Lionel was seven, he was old enough to join the Newell's junior teams, as his father and brother had done. Lionel was joined by other very good young players, and their team became almost unbeatable. Because most of the team members were born in 1987, they were nicknamed "the

'87 Machine." They won game after game; in one 10–0 win, Lionel scored eight of the goals!

Lionel's grandmother Celia died when he

was ten, and he started pointing to the sky with two fingers after every goal to remember her. He had a lot of chances to point—Lionel scored 234 goals in 176 games with Newell's.

As Lionel got older, Jorge wanted to make sure that his son had a chance to play at the top level. He made videos of Lionel's best plays. Videos were also made of Lionel juggling an orange and a tennis ball hundreds of times in a row with his feet, showing off his great abilities. He gathered videos of Lionel dribbling around several players before kicking goals. Jorge sent the tapes to pro teams in Argentina, Spain, and Italy.

When Lionel was eleven, however, his doctors discovered the reason he was so small. There was a problem with a chemical in his body called a growth hormone. The doctors said that Lionel could get shots of medicine that might help correct this. He would have to take the shots almost every day, and the medicine was very expensive. The family was worried that they could not afford the treatment.

Then one of the teams that had seen Jorge's tapes of Lionel contacted the family. Futbol Club (FC) Barcelona in Spain is one of the most famous soccer clubs in the world. They asked Jorge and Lionel to fly to Spain so that Lionel could try out for Barcelona's youth teams.

In Spain, Lionel spent several weeks practicing and working out with other players, including some of Barcelona's first-team international superstars.

Barcelona club director Carles Rexach finally got to see Lionel play in a game in October 2000. After just a few minutes watching, he was convinced. Lionel and Jorge went back to Argentina. Carles Rexach and Jorge continued to discuss the deal that would bring Lionel back to play for Spain. At one point, Rexach even wrote out a famous promise to sign Lionel . . . on a napkin!

Once the deal was set, Lionel and most of his family moved to Spain in 2001. Lionel cried during the long flight across the Atlantic Ocean. He knew it was the right move for him, but he was going to miss his friends and his neighborhood. In Barcelona, the team found the Messis an apartment and helped Jorge find a job, too. They also paid for the medical treatments that Lionel still needed.

Lionel began training and studying at Barcelona's La Masia, an academy for the team's many young players. He was still very shy and it took him a long time to fit in with the other, mostly older, boys. He also had to learn a new language, as most people in Barcelona spoke Catalan, not Spanish, as Lionel did in Argentina. Eventually, he found a way to connect with other kids by playing tabletop soccer, called foosball.

He also found Argentine restaurants in Barcelona where he could enjoy food that he loved from back home.

In the summer of 2001, everyone except Jorge and Lionel moved back to Argentina. Lionel said later that he would often cry himself to sleep because he missed his mother and his siblings so much.

Lionel was moving quickly through Barcelona's several layers of youth teams, such as Under-16 and Under-19. In 2003, he played at five different age group levels! In 2004, he played his first game with Barcelona's top team, FC Barcelona. Lionel was only seventeen, the second youngest ever to play for the famous club since its founding in 1899. Lionel saved the jersey from that game to send home to Argentina to his mother.

CHAPTER 2
Barcelona

Lionel had made it to the top team as a professional. Like other international stars, however, he also played for his country's team. By 2005, when Lionel turned eighteen, Argentina wanted him to play for their national team. He was called up for the under-twenty (known as the U-20) World Cup, which was being held in the Netherlands that year. This tournament is open only to players under twenty years old. Messi was the biggest star in the event, scoring six goals. His two penalty-kick goals in the final helped Argentina defeat Nigeria 2–1. Messi was named the top player of the tournament.

Later that summer, he played in his first game

for Argentina's senior national team. It did not go as well as the Under-20s. In a friendly against Hungary, Lionel was brought on as a substitute in the second half. Just two minutes later, a defender tried to stop Lionel as he dribbled. Lionel swung out an arm that hit the defender in the throat. He was not trying to hurt his opponent, but the referee gave Lionel a red card and kicked him out of the game. Lionel cried in the locker room afterward, as his teammates tried to cheer him up.

Later that year, Lionel flew home to Argentina to help Antonela, his childhood friend. She had lost her best friend to a car accident, and Lionel went to comfort her. They soon began dating, though she remained in Rosario, while Lionel traveled back to Barcelona.

Over the next three years, Lionel became a star for Barcelona. He grew more comfortable living in Spain. He was making plenty of money, too.

He helped his family back in Argentina, and also bought houses for himself and his father. But his focus was always on the games.

In 2007, he scored a famous goal during a game against Getafe, another team in La Liga, the top Spanish soccer league. Lionel got the ball about midfield. He then dribbled more than sixty yards toward the goal. He went around or through five defenders, then dribbled around the goalie and kicked the ball into the goal with his right foot. It was an incredible goal, and fans around the world still watch it over and over online.

During a summer trip to the United States, Lionel visited a children's hospital in Boston. He met several children with cancer, including the daughter of a man from Argentina. Lionel was very moved by what he saw there. Even though he was only twenty, he was making tens of millions of dollars playing soccer and advertising products.

Club and Country

Around the world, professional soccer players can play for two different kinds of teams. Their main team is the professional club that pays them. An athlete can play for a club in any

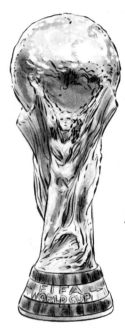

country. A player like Lionel Messi from Argentina or Rose Lavelle of the United States can play in a pro league in Spain, France, England, or elsewhere. Each club plays in a league based in one country, such as FC Barcelona for Spain's La Liga. In some countries, there are dozens or hundreds of professional soccer clubs. National teams, on the

The World Cup trophy

other hand, include only players who are citizens of one country. The teams take part in tournaments, such as for the championship of a continent, or in the World Cup or the Women's World Cup, which are played every four years. They also play each other in "friendlies," which are practice or exhibition games that are not part of a tournament.

To share some of that wealth, Lionel and his family started the Leo Messi Foundation. The foundation is run by Lionel's brother Rodrigo. They focus on helping children, donating to children's hospitals in Argentina and Spain. The foundation also gives money to youth soccer groups in Argentina, with a focus on special needs athletes.

In 2008, Lionel led Argentina into the Olympic Games in Beijing. Men's Olympic soccer teams are made up mainly of players twenty-three and under; Lionel was still just twenty-one. Argentina beat South American rival Brazil in the semifinal. In the gold-medal match, Argentina held on for a 1–0 win over Nigeria.

Before the 2009 season, Lionel received a special honor. The FC Barcelona star Ronaldinho was leaving the team, and he gave his number ten jersey to Lionel. That number usually goes to a team's most important and famous player. Lionel has worn number ten for nearly every team since then.

In 2008–2009, wearing number ten, Lionel led Barcelona to one of the most amazing seasons in soccer history. The team won six trophies. They won the La Liga championship, the Copa del Rey, the Spanish Super Cup, the European Super Cup, and the Champions League. And in December 2009, they won the FIFA Club World Cup. No team had ever won all six in a single calendar year. Lionel scored thirty-eight goals for the team, and earned his first Ballon d'Or (Golden Ball), a French award for the best player in the world.

Winning for Barcelona was important, but Lionel wanted to help his country be a world champion, too. At the 2010 World Cup, Lionel was made the Argentina team captain for the first time. However, he and his teammates lost to

Germany 4–0 in the quarterfinals. Lionel cried in the locker room after the game.

Not long after the World Cup ended, Lionel made a trip to Haiti in his role as a UNICEF ambassador. (UNICEF stands for the United Nations International Children's Emergency Fund.) In January 2010, that country had been hit by a terrible earthquake. Lionel's visit was to call attention to the ongoing need for people to help Haiti recover.

In 2012, Lionel did something no soccer player had ever done. Counting all of the games he had played for both Barcelona and Argentina, he scored ninety-one goals. That broke a record of eighty-five set in 1972 by Germany's Gerd Müller.

Another highlight of that year was the birth of Lionel's son Thiago, his first child with Antonela. Thiago helped Lionel learn to focus on more than just soccer. "I've adopted a different approach since my first son was born," he said. "It made me stop burying myself in my career."

Lionel Messi and Antonela holding their firstborn son, Thiago

After Lionel earned his fourth straight Ballon d'Or in late 2012, he said, "I prefer winning titles with the team over individual awards or scoring more goals. I am more concerned about being a good person than being the best footballer in the world."

CHAPTER 3
Highs and Lows

Lionel and Argentina had another chance to win soccer's top prize at the 2014 World Cup. Lionel scored four goals in the team's first three games. And although he did win the Golden Ball as the top player in the tournament, it was not the World Cup, the trophy he really wanted.

Later in 2014, Lionel became the all-time leading goal-scorer in Spain's La Liga history with his 252nd goal for Barcelona. The league had been around since 1929, and the record he broke had been set in 1955—Lionel was now making history every time he scored.

The 2014–2015 season was another triumph for Barcelona. The team won the Copa del Rey, La Liga, and the Champions League. Lionel scored forty-three goals and his eighteen assists led La Liga. In the summer, though, Lionel and Argentina fell short at another major international tournament. Argentina lost to Chile in the final match of the Copa América, the championship of South America.

Later in 2015, Lionel and Antonela welcomed another son, Mateo, and Lionel won another Ballon d'Or as the world's top player. But then came more international disappointment. In the 2016 Copa América, Lionel and Argentina lost again to Chile in the final. The game was tied and went to a penalty-kick shootout—and Lionel missed his shot. In tears after the game, Lionel was so disappointed that he said, "My time with the national team has finished." (By the end of the year, he changed his mind and would play for Argentina again.)

Then, just two weeks after the game, Lionel and his father, Jorge, were in court in Spain. The government had convicted them of not paying enough taxes on the money Lionel earned. The Messis had to pay a large fine. "I trusted my dad and my lawyers," Lionel said. But the court said he was responsible for paying his taxes.

In June 2017, soccer stars from around the world, along with Messi family and friends, celebrated Lionel and Antonela's wedding in Rosario. Newspapers called it Argentina's "wedding of the century." In 2018, the couple had a third son, Ciro.

Lionel and Barcelona won La Liga again in 2018 and 2019, but they failed to win the top prize in the next two seasons. However, in the summer of 2021, Lionel did get a big trophy for Argentina. The 2020 Copa América was moved to 2021 due to the COVID-19 pandemic. (Lionel's foundation donated more than a million dollars to Argentina for pandemic support.)

Lionel and Antonela's wedding, 2017

In the tournament, Lionel scored four goals as Argentina made it to the final game against the host country, Brazil. Argentina's defense kept a powerful Brazil team—led by superstar forward Neymar—from scoring. Brazil, meanwhile, shut down Lionel. But his teammate Ángel Di María did score in the first half. When the final whistle blew, Lionel cried with joy. He was named the top player in the tournament, and as captain, he raised his first major international trophy. It was also the first time since 1993 that Argentina had won the Copa América.

The joy of that moment was soon overtaken with sad news. La Liga rules made it impossible for Barcelona to sign Lionel to another contract. The team had gone over a salary limit put on them by the league, and they had spent too much money on other players. Lionel even offered to cut his salary in half, but it was not enough. After twenty years, 672 goals, ten La Liga championships, and four Champions League trophies, Lionel had to leave the team he had been with since he was thirteen. He was now thirty-three.

He was very sad at the final press conference. "We thought we would be staying here in Barcelona. But today, we have to say goodbye to all of this."

In August 2021, Lionel announced that he had signed to play in France, for the famous club Paris Saint-Germain (PSG). Because the club was already home to a famous number ten—Neymar—Lionel returned to his original FC Barcelona number—number thirty.

CHAPTER 4
Finally, a World Champion

Along with Neymar, Lionel's new PSG teammates included the French star Kylian Mbappé. Together, the trio made the club huge

favorites to win the French league, known as Ligue 1. And the team of superstars did just that, winning the 2022 championship. In the final road game of the season, Lionel scored. It was his 496th goal while playing for a club in Europe, breaking a record set by Cristiano Ronaldo of Portugal, one of Lionel's rivals for best player in the world.

Lionel Messi, Neymar, and Kylian Mbappé
on the field together at the Ligue 1 2022 championship

In November and December 2022, the World Cup was held in the nation of Qatar. The event is usually held in the summer, but extreme heat in the Middle Eastern country moved the games to cooler months. Lionel had announced earlier that this would be his last World Cup. It was his last chance to win the biggest prize in soccer.

The tournament began with a shock. In Argentina's first game, Lionel scored a goal, but his team lost to Saudi Arabia 2–1. It was one of the biggest upsets in World Cup history. But Lionel rallied his teammates to beat Mexico and Poland, and they advanced to the next round.

In a win over Australia, Lionel scored again and Argentina moved on. In the quarterfinals, Lionel scored yet again, but Argentina let the Netherlands score very late in extra time to tie the score. Argentina had to win on a penalty-kick shootout.

In the semifinals, Lionel continued his amazing play. He made a first-half penalty kick to become Argentina's all-time World Cup goal-scorer. Lionel scored again late in the game and his team beat Croatia 3–0. That set up a final between Argentina and France that turned into one of the best games in soccer history. Both teams featured megastars—Lionel and Mbappé. Billions of people around the world tuned in to watch the action.

In the first half, Lionel scored the game's first goal on a penalty kick. Di María added a second goal for Argentina. France looked like it was beaten, but Mbappé came through. With less than ten minutes left in the game, he made a penalty kick of his own. Only two minutes later, the French star blasted a long right-footed shot into the net—tie game!

In extra time, Lionel scored yet again. Ahead 3–2, Argentina was just minutes away from a championship when another penalty was called. Mbappé scored the penalty kick, and extra time ended with a 3–3 tie.

In the penalty shootout, Lionel went first and scored. But so did Mbappé. France then missed two of the kicks, one of which was saved by Argentina's goalie, Emiliano Martínez. When Lionel's teammate Gonzalo Montiel made his kick, Argentina became the World Cup champion!

Lionel became the first player to score in all five rounds of a World Cup. He wound up with seven goals and won his second World Cup Golden Ball as the top player. As the team captain, he proudly held the World Cup trophy amid his teammates as confetti poured down!

In a letter posted online to his fans, Lionel remembered all the times he and Argentina had come close before. He thanked everyone who had helped him, from his earliest days at

Grandoli to his teammates in Spain and France. He concluded by writing, "Failure is often part of the journey . . . and without disappointments it is impossible for success to come. Thank you very much from the bottom of my heart! Let's go Argentina!"

FIFA WORLD CUP

World Cup celebration, 2022

CHAPTER 5
Messi to Miami

Lionel returned to PSG and helped them win another title in 2023. But he had a big surprise for his fans around the world. In June, he announced that he was joining a new team— Inter Miami FC of Major League Soccer in the United States.

Lionel could have gone to any team in the world. A team in Saudi Arabia supposedly offered him more than a billion dollars to play there. But Lionel wanted a good place for his family. Soccer is a big deal in the United States, but nowhere near as big as in Europe or South America. Why Inter Miami FC?

Lionel owned a home in Miami and enjoyed the city's great weather. He also liked that he could go out with his family without being swarmed by fans and photographers. Lionel knew he would have a chance to help pro soccer grow in the United States.

He arrived in June and in his first game against Mexico's Cruz Azul, made that first game-winning free kick. That was just the start. Over the next five weeks, he led Miami to win after win in the Leagues Cup. He scored eleven goals and had eight assists in his first eleven games with the team. One of them was another free kick that tied a game with very little time left. Another goal came from thirty-six yards, one of the longest of his career.

Ticket prices for Miami's games soared. Millions of people watched every game on TV. The Major League Soccer team's Instagram account grew from one million followers to fifteen million followers. (Meanwhile, Lionel's Instagram following was the third biggest in the world with more than *490* million followers!)

With every defender focused on him each game, Lionel came through over and over again. It helped that former Barcelona teammates Jordi Alba and Sergio Busquets had also signed with the team to join Lionel in Miami.

For his part, Lionel loved playing in Miami, especially because he had his family with him. He even changed his fingers-to-heaven goal celebration because of them. After some early goals, fans saw Lionel make a series of superhero poses from Thor, Black Panther, and Spider-Man. Lionel explained that they were for his children, with whom he loved watching superhero movies!

And so Miami, a team that was in last place before Lionel arrived, reached the championship match of the Leagues Cup. In the first half against Nashville, Lionel got the ball at the top of the penalty box. He dribbled past two defenders and cracked a left-footed shot. It flew past two other defenders and the goalie into the net!

Lionel Messi doing the Black Panther pose
for his children after scoring a goal

The game ended in a 1–1 tie. The penalty-kick shootout went to the last round, and Miami won 10–9 when its goalie, Drake Callender, stopped the final Nashville shot. Miami won the Cup! Lionel's teammates tossed him in the air in celebration!

On August 26, 2023, Lionel played in his first regular-season MLS game for Miami. Tired from a busy month, he only came on as a substitute. But, of course, he scored, as Miami beat the New York Red Bulls. In October, Lionel received his eighth Ballon d'Or, adding to his all-time record total.

The big wins in Miami and this major award capped off one of the most remarkable years of Lionel's incredible career. What else can the world's greatest soccer player do?

Timeline of Lionel Messi's Life

1987	Lionel is born in Rosario, Argentina, on June 24
1994	Joins the Newell's Old Boys soccer club in Rosario
2001	Moves to Spain to join the youth academy at FC Barcelona
2004	Plays in his first game for Barcelona's top team
2008	Wins Olympic gold medal playing for Argentina in Beijing, China
2009	Wins the first of his record eight Ballon d'Or awards as the world's best player
2012	Sets a new world record by scoring ninety-one goals in a year
	With girlfriend, Antonela Roccuzzo, has son, Thiago
2014	Loses World Cup final against Germany
2015	Lionel and Antonela have another son, Mateo
2017	Marries Antonela in Rosario
2018	Lionel and Antonela have a third son, Ciro
2021	Wins Copa América with Argentina
	Moves from FC Barcelona to Paris Saint-Germain (PSG) in the French league
2022	Wins World Cup with Argentina; awarded Ballon d'Or
2023	Moves from PSG to Inter Miami of Major League Soccer; leads Miami to victory in the Leagues Cup

Timeline of the World

1984 — The first Apple Macintosh computer is sold

1990 — The Hubble Space Telescope is launched, helping bring new views of the distant universe

1994 — The Channel Tunnel, connecting England and France, opens for business

2001 — Terrorist attacks on September 11 in the United States kill nearly 3,000 people and destroy the World Trade Center towers in New York City

2005 — Hurricane Katrina causes huge damage on the Gulf Coast of the United States

2007 — *Diary of a Wimpy Kid*, the first book in a popular series by Jeff Kinney, is published

2008 — Barack Obama is elected as the first Black US president

2010 — Thirty-three trapped miners are rescued from a deep mine in Chile

2014 — Malala Yousafzai becomes the youngest Nobel Peace Prize winner for her work in Pakistan on behalf of women and girls in education

2016 — Great Britain votes to leave the European Union, a process nicknamed "Brexit"

2019 — Scientists reveal the first image of a black hole in distant space, taken with the Event Horizon Telescope

2022 — Russia invades the country of Ukraine

Bibliography

*Books for young readers

*Anderson, Josh. *Lionel Messi vs. Pelé: Who Would Win?*
Minneapolis: Lerner Books, 2024.

Bader, Bonnie. *What Is the World Cup?* New York: Penguin
Workshop, 2018.

Balagué, Guillem. *Messi* (revised edition). London: Seven Dials,
2023.

*Bryan, J.J. *Play Soccer Like Lionel Messi*. Minneapolis: Gray Duck
Creative Works, 2023.

*Buckley, James Jr. *Who Is Cristiano Ronaldo?* New York: Penguin
Workshop, 2022.

Faccio, Leonardo. *Messi: A Biography*. New York: Anchor Books,
2012.

*Stabler, David. *Meet Lionel Messi: World Cup Superstars*.
Minneapolis: Lerner Sports, 2022.